THIS WALKER BOOK BELONGS TO:

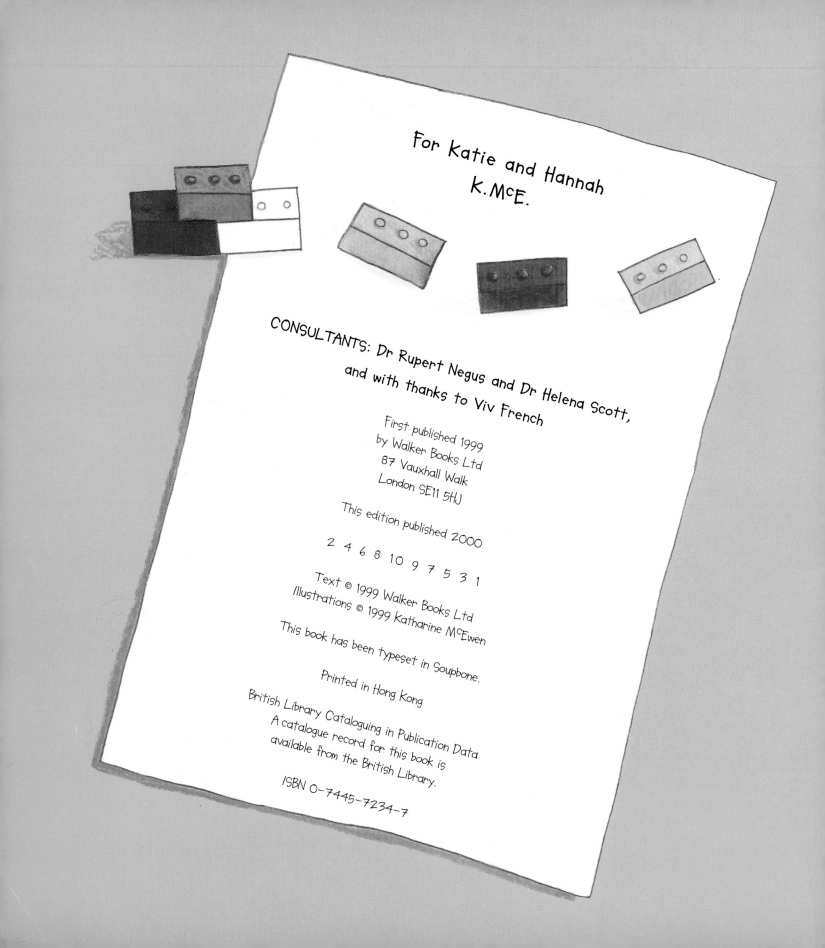

For Katie and Hannah
K. McE.

CONSULTANTS: Dr Rupert Negus and Dr Helena Scott,
and with thanks to Viv French

First published 1999
by Walker Books Ltd
87 Vauxhall Walk
London SE11 5HJ

This edition published 2000

2 4 6 8 10 9 7 5 3 1

Text © 1999 Walker Books Ltd
Illustrations © 1999 Katharine McEwen

This book has been typeset in Soupbone.

Printed in Hong Kong

British Library Cataloguing in Publication Data
A catalogue record for this book is
available from the British Library.

ISBN 0-7445-7234-7

I KNOW HOW MY CELLS MAKE ME GROW

KATE ROWAN

illustrated by

KATHARINE McEWEN

WALKER BOOKS
AND SUBSIDIARIES
LONDON • BOSTON • SYDNEY

"Help!" squeaked Sam.

"I'm stuck! My jumper's shrunk!"

"Oh, no it hasn't," said Mum.
"You've been getting bigger.
Let's get that jumper off
and have a look at
your height chart."

Sam stood against the chart.

"Wow!" he said.

"I'm halfway up the
dinosaur's neck!"

"Goodness!" said Mum. "You've grown
4 whole centimetres since I last measured you."

"I know why I'm growing so fast," said Sam.
"It's all the exercises
we've been doing in gym."

Mum smiled. "They may have helped a bit,
but mainly it's because parts of your
body are getting bigger. Your **bones**
and your **muscles** and your **skin**
are growing — so you are, too."

9

"I know about **bones** and **muscles** and **skin**," said Sam.

"**Bones** hold me up. If I didn't have any I'd be all floppy, like a tent with no poles.

And **muscles** let me move around. And my **skin** protects my insides from germs and stuff."

10

"That's right," said Mum. "Come on — let's get this room tidy before breakfast."

"OK," said Sam.
"But how do **bones** and **muscles** and **skin** grow? Do they stretch like rubber bands?"

"Not exactly," Mum said. "Most of your body is made of tiny things called **cells**. When you grow, it's because your **bone cells** are making more **bone cells**, and your **muscle cells** are making more **muscle cells**, and..."

"I know! I know!"
shouted Sam.

"My **skin cells** are
making more **skin cells**!"

"Exactly," said Mum.

"You've got lots of different kinds of **cell**
in your body — about 200 I think —
and each kind is a different shape.

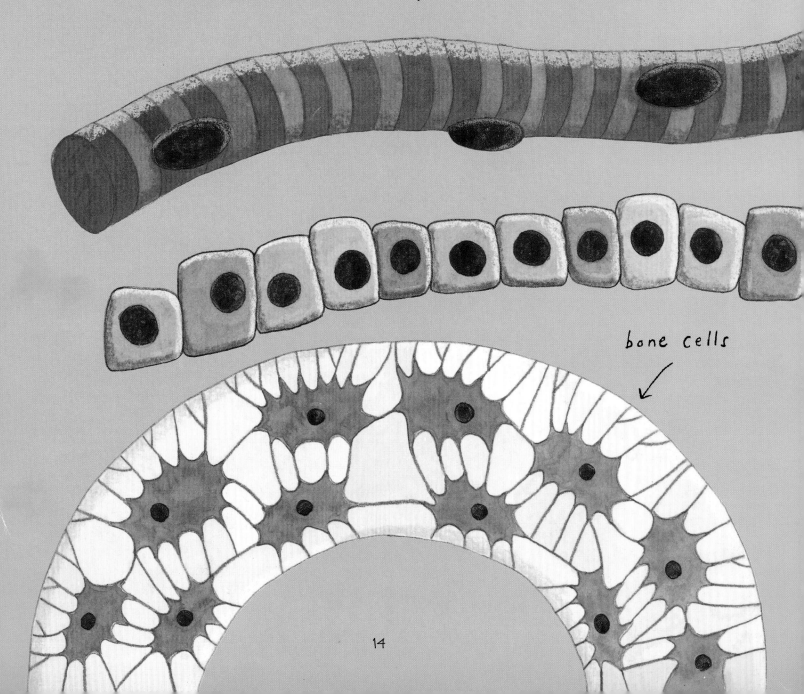

bone cells

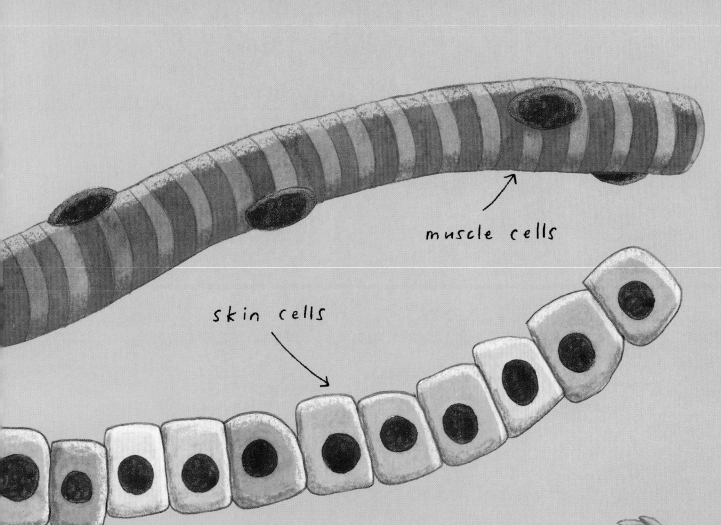

muscle cells

skin cells

Some of your **muscle cells** look
like long stripy strings, for example.
And some kinds of **skin cell**
are shaped like little cubes.
And there are **bone cells** that
look just like spiky blobs."

"Weird!" said Sam.
"But how do you know
they look like that?
Can you see them?"

microscope

"Not easily," said Mum.
"They're too small
to see just with
your eyes. You'd need
a microscope to look
at them properly."

Mum grinned. "There is a kind of **cell** that you can see, though — the yolk of a bird's egg. In fact, the yolk of an ostrich's egg is the biggest kind of **cell** in the world!"

Mum picked up Sam's old jumper.

"Your **cells** are a bit like the stitches in this jumper," she said.
"Each one is very small, but when they join together they make something much bigger."

"Like building bricks," Sam said.

"That's right," said Mum.
"Only your **cells** are all
much much smaller than
bricks or stitches."

"Yeah," said Sam.
"So I must be made
of millions and
millions of **cells**."

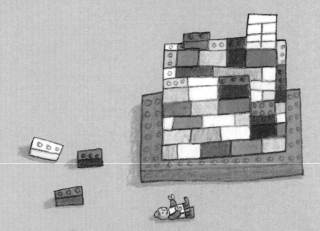

"BILLIONS and BILLIONS," said Mum. "There are about 10,000 million **cells** in just one of your thumbs!"

Sam peered at his thumb.
"I still don't see how my body
makes more **cells**, though.
Where do they come from?"

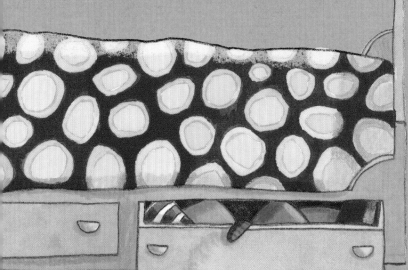

"Well," said Mum, "what **cells** do is make copies of themselves. It's incredibly clever.
Each **cell** starts by growing a little bigger.

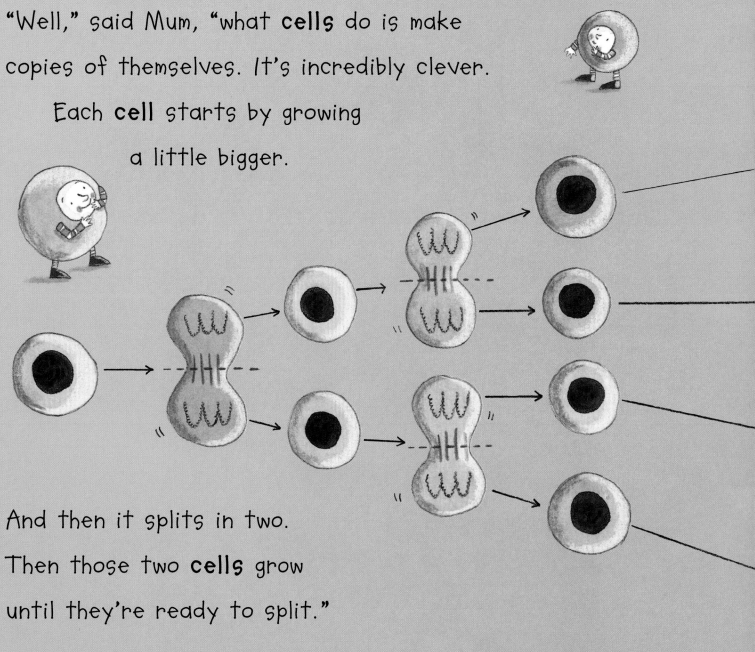

And then it splits in two.
Then those two **cells** grow
until they're ready to split."

"And they make four **cells**,"
Sam said. "Two times two is four."

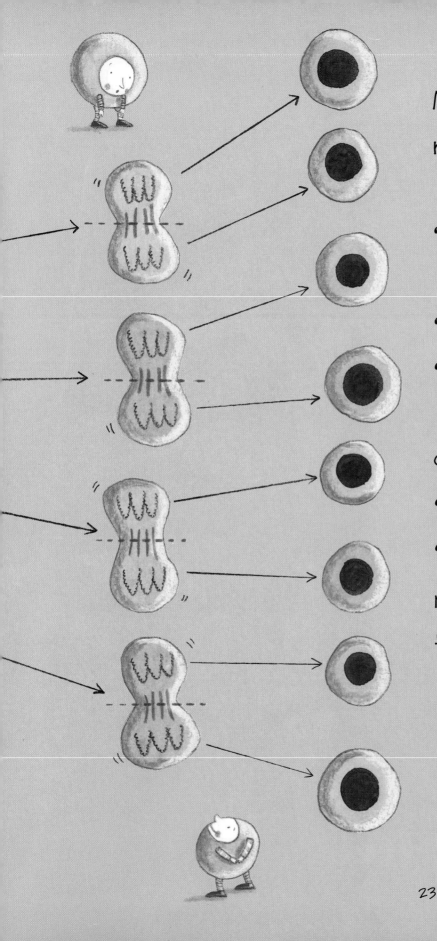

Mum smiled. "And what comes next? Two times four is?"

"Eight!" yelled Sam.

"Good," said Mum.
"And two times eight is...?"

Sam grinned.

"A lot," he said.
"Do **cells** go on making more and more **cells** for ever and ever then?"

23

"Some do," said Mum. "Some kinds of **cell** are always wearing out and dying, so your body needs to make new ones to replace them.

You lose millions of **skin cells** every day, for example. They get rubbed off by your clothes or by washing, and lots just fall off by themselves."

24

"But not all your **cells** carry on making
more **cells** for ever and ever," explained Mum,
"or you'd go on growing for ever and ever!
When you get to about seventeen or eighteen,
for instance, your **bone cells** will slow
right down and almost stop making
new **cells**. And that's when
you'll stop getting taller."

"Have all your **cells** slowed down?"
Sam asked.

Mum laughed.
"Well, I'm certainly not
growing any taller!"

"I wish all my **cells**
would go on growing,"
Sam said. "Then I'd get
to be as tall as a
Tyrannosaurus Rex!"

"You'd better hurry up and help me put these things away so we can get on and have breakfast then," said Mum. "**Cells** need feeding so they can work properly!"

And she began to close the chest drawers.

"MUM!" gasped Sam, and he giggled.

"You're bursting out of your trousers!"

Sam

cells

Index

Look up the pages to find out about all these cell things.